CHURCH MUSIC SOCIETY PUBLICATION: 023A
Hon. General Editor: Richard Lyne

for the Choir and Congregation of St. Mary's Church, North Leigh,

Saint Mary's Mass

Music by ANTHONY CÆSAR

Kyrie

Gloria

Allegretto giocoso

Glo - ry to God in the high - est, and peace to his peo-ple on earth. Lord God, hea-ven-ly King, al-migh-ty God and Fa - ther, we wor - ship you, we give you thanks, we praise you for your glo - ry.

Lord Je - sus Christ, on - ly Son of the Fa - ther, Lord God, Lamb of God, you take a - way the sin of the world: have mer - cy on us: you are seat - ed at the right hand of the Fa - ther: re - ceive our prayer.

Tempo primo

For you — a-lone are the Ho - ly One, you a-lone are the Lord, —

cresc. *f*

you a-lone are the Most High, Je - sus Christ, with the Ho - ly Spi - rit,

allargando *ff*

in the glo-ry of God — the Fa - ther. A - men. A - men.

Gospel Responses

mf

Glo - ry to Christ — our Sa - viour.

mf *f*

Praise — to Christ — our Lord. —

Sanctus – Benedictus

Andante solenne *pp*

Ho - ly, Ho - ly, Ho - ly Lord, God — of pow'r and

più mosso *mf* *f*

might, heav'n — and earth are full — of your glo - ry. Ho-san-na in the

mf

high - est. Bless - ed is he who comes — in the name — of the

f *ff*

Lord. Ho-san - na in the high-est, Ho - san-na in the high - est.

Acclamations

Agnus Dei

Acknowledgment

The *Gloria,* the *Sanctus,* the *Benedictus* and the *Agnus Dei* from *The Order for Holy Communion Rite A* from the Alternative Service Book 1980 are © International Consultation on English Texts and are reproduced with permission of the Central Board of Finance of the Church of England.

ISBN 0-19-395363-3

Origination by Jeanne Fisher, Ludlow, Shropshire
Printed by Halstan & Co. Ltd., Amersham, Bucks

Pack of 10 copies
Not available separately